Cath Senker | **How to get ahead in**

Catering

www.raintreepublishers.co.uk

Visit our website to find out more information about **Raintree** books.

To order:

 Phone 44 (0) 1865 888113

 Send a fax to 44 (0) 1865 314091

 Visit the Raintree bookshop at **www.raintreepublishers.co.uk** to browse our catalogue and order online.

First published in Great Britain by Raintree, Halley Court, Jordan Hill, Oxford OX2 8EJ, part of Harcourt Education.
Raintree is a registered trademark of Harcourt Education Ltd.

Editorial: Melanie Waldron, Lucy Beevor, and Kate Buckingham
Design: David Poole and Calcium
Illustrations: Geoff Ward
Picture Research: Ruth Blair and Maria Joannou
Production: Huseyin Sami

Originated by Chroma Graphics
Printed and bound in China by South China Printing Company

10 digit ISBN 1 406 20443 9
13 digit ISBN 978 1 4062 0443 8

11 10 09 08 07
10 9 8 7 6 5 4 3 2 1

British Library Cataloguing in Publication Data

Senker, Cath
How to Get Ahead in Catering
647.9'5'02341
A full catalogue record for this book is available from the British Library.

Acknowledgements

The publishers would like to thank the following for permission to reproduce photographs: Alamy Images pp.**12** (Daniel Templeton), **6** (Danita Delimont), **7** (David Hancock), **24** (Mark Scott), **37** (Steffan Hill); Anthony Blake Picture Library pp. **49, 5, 30** (Dominic Dibbs), **18** (Joerg Lehmann); Corbis pp. **36** (Ed Quinn), **33** (Owen Franken); Getty Images pp. **20** (Phonica), **22** (Stone/Bob Thomas), **14** (Stone/Judith Haeusler), **39** (Stone/Rene Sheret), **25** (Taxi/Hans Neleman), **16** (Taxi/Holly Harris), **48** (Taxi/Patrick Molnar), **34** (The Images Bank/Simon Watson); Imagestate p. **23** (Bay Hippisley); Lonely Planet Images p.**47** (Greg Elms); Report Digital pp.**41** (Duncan Phillips), **29, 44** (John Harris), **8, 11, 42** (Roy Peters); Rex Features pp. **9** (Garo/Phanie), **27** (Richard Saker), **10** (Julian Makey).

Cover photograph of poached pears, reproduced with permission of Photolibrary/Foodpix/Jung Richard.

The author would like to thank the following for their help in the preparation of this book: Mohammed Asaduzzaman; Brian Bell, City College, Brighton; Keir Bottrill; John Cadien and Springboard UK (www.springboarduk.org.uk. Search for John Cadien); David Herranz; Dave Lonners; James Mason; Jenny Matthews; Jane McKenna; Vanessa Nickerson; Nuala O'Brien; Ian Sillett; Colin Vetters and Alan Wark, Paisley Grammar School, Glasgow.

Every effort has been made to contact copyright holders of any material reproduced in this book. Any omissions will be rectified in subsequent printings if notice is given to the publishers.

Disclaimer

Contents

Words appearing in the text in bold, **like this**, are explained in the glossary.

Why work in catering?

With so many people eating outside the home every day, there are lots of jobs that involve preparing and serving food and drink. You could be working anywhere from a small, cosy café or restaurant, to a busy university canteen or even a fancy top-class hotel. Catering is not just about cooking. You might prefer to work with customers, serving their refreshments. Or if you are more into organizing than preparing and serving food, there are plenty of management careers available.

CATERING CAREERS QUIZ

Which area of the catering business might be for you? Try this fun careers quiz for starters.

1 Are you fit and healthy, and happy to be on your feet for much of the day?
a) Yes, I like to be moving about and I have plenty of energy.
b) No, give me a comfy office with a phone and computer.

2 Do you like working with your hands and enjoy preparing meals?
a) Yes. At home, they can't keep me out of the kitchen.
b) Pass that take-away pizza, please!

3 Do you enjoy working in a team?
a) Yes, I like sharing ideas and enjoy the company.
b) No, I prefer to work on my own **initiative**.

4 Are you an outgoing, lively person who can get on with all kinds of people?
a) Yes, I'm a "people" person.
b) No, I'm quite shy and quiet.

5 Do you like working with customers?
a) Yes, I enjoy keeping people happy.
b) No, I can't possibly smile all day long.

6 Do you like dressing smartly and would you be happy to wear a uniform?

a) Yes, I like to dress the part for work.

b) No, I want to dress how I like.

7 Do you have good keyboard skills and enjoy using IT?

a) Yes, that's me. I've got a head for figures too.

b) No, I don't even like email.

8 Do you like to organize and manage tasks?

a) Yes, I'm always making lists! I'd like to learn business skills.

b) No, I'm hopelessly forgetful and disorganized.

Quiz results

Of course, choosing a career isn't as simple as this. But if you answered "a" to questions 1–4, then a career making food could be for you (see chapters 1 and 3). If you answered "a" to questions 1 and 3–6, then you might enjoy serving food and caring for customers (see chapter 3). If your answers were mostly "a", including to questions 7 and 8, a career in catering management might suit you (see chapter 5).

below: *A waiter and waitress prepare to serve attractively presented starters.*

Chapter 1

Making meals

Catering involves making and serving meals for people on a regular basis. About two-thirds of the business is in the commercial sector – making food to sell for a profit. It includes catering on a large scale for workplaces, hotels, fast-food outlets, cruise ships, holiday and leisure centres, pubs, clubs, and restaurants. There are also smaller catering outlets, such as tea rooms, little coffee bars, and smart restaurants with just a few tables. Then there is catering for people on the move – on trains, buses, and aeroplanes.

Commercial catering

In this sector, you will tend to work long hours and will need to be flexible. You don't know exactly when hungry, thirsty people will turn up – or how many will come through the door. You may have to work overtime at short notice. Also, you will probably have to be quite flexible about the work you do. You might be a trainee chef, but if the kitchen assistants are run off their feet, you could be helping to scrub dirty pans.

Get ahead!

Find out about commercial catering jobs in your local area. There are probably fast-food restaurants and cafes in chain stores. If you live in an area popular with tourists, you probably have hotels, guest houses, and restaurants nearby.

right: *A career in catering could take you around the world on a cruise ship.*

Hungry for change?

The catering industry provides a world of opportunities to travel and work in different locations. You could get a job as an airline steward or even on a cruise ship! The skills are very transferable – what you learn in one job will be useful in other catering posts. You can start in one kind of establishment and easily move on to different catering jobs.

below: *Airline stewards spend their working hours above the clouds!*

CASE STUDY

Dave Lonners is an airline steward.

I work for a large airline company. I steward mostly in the first-class cabin on long-haul flights. We are there to make sure the passengers are safe and to look after them during their flight. The food is prepared by chefs on the ground, but the way we deliver it to the customers is very important. The stewards assemble the food, heat it up, and add the final touches. For our first-class customers, we make the pasta and toss the salads. I have to know about the food I'm serving, and I have been on courses to learn about wine. Some people specialize in wine and become on-board sommeliers (wine waiters).

Being an airline steward is like having a new job each day. You're working with different staff and customers. If you're outgoing, have a sense of humour, and would like to travel the world in style, this could be for you.

The non-profit sector

There are plenty of catering jobs in the **non-profit sector** too. Wherever you live, there are likely to be hospitals and schools, and possibly nursing homes too. You may live close to colleges or universities that have canteens and snack bars for their staff and students. As in the commercial sector, you will find a variety of large and small catering outlets.

Hospitals

The biggest provider of meals in the UK catering industry is the National Health Service (NHS). Hospitals run a huge catering organization to serve food to all the patients as well as the staff and visitors. This can mean providing meals day and night for hundreds or even thousands of people. Some hospitals have an on-site kitchen where meals are cooked. The meals are then brought round the wards on trolleys.

In some NHS trusts (organizations that run hospitals), a catering system is used. Catering systems are increasingly being used in both the profit and non-profit sectors. They are popular with large catering companies and chain restaurants as well as hospitals. Instead of allowing the chef in each kitchen to choose the menu, the dishes are made in one central location.

If you work in the central kitchen, you have to follow precise recipes and present the food in a particular way. You will need to know about health and hygiene to ensure the meals do not spoil, but you won't be learning creative cooking. Once the meals are made, they are either frozen or chilled and taken to the various hospitals in the trust. There, the kitchen workers heat them up in the hospital kitchen, ready for serving.

left: *Hospitals need caterers to provide good, healthy food.*

Do you like hospital food?

There have always been jokes about how terrible hospital food is. The Better Hospital Food Programme, first introduced in 2001, has raised the standards, but there is still much room for improvement. Good-quality food helps patients to recover, so hospital catering is very important too.

WORKING HOURS

When you are thinking about which sector to work in, think about the working hours you would prefer. In the non-profit sector, hours are generally more regular and shorter than in the commercial sector. For example, if you are serving in an office canteen, you may finish mid-afternoon after clearing up from lunch. Similarly, if you work in school catering, you will usually finish before school is out for the day. If you work in a school, you will benefit from having school holidays. But remember, the longer hours in the commercial sector mean you are likely to earn more money and gain experience more quickly.

above: *Healthy food can help sick and injured people get better more quickly.*

School catering

As in hospitals, school meals are often provided by catering companies. The dinners are cooked centrally by the catering company and then brought to the schools in the area. If you are working in the school kitchen, you are most likely to be reheating and serving prepared meals. In lots of ways, this is similar to any large-scale catering job.

When the chips are down...

In recent years, though, there has been a big debate in the UK about young people's diets. Many rely on ready-cooked meals and fast food, and rarely eat home-made dishes. TV chef Jamie Oliver has led a campaign to improve school dinners. He has encouraged schools to stop serving ready-made meals and cook dinners from scratch every day. Now many schools are returning to on-site cooking in their school kitchen, using fresh vegetables and fruit. So a job in school catering can be a real cooking job.

below: *Jamie Oliver serving school pupils healthy, tasty food.*

above: *School meals are now often freshly prepared every day.*

CASE STUDY

Nuala O'Brien works as a kitchen supervisor.

I've been cooking since I was a child. Of the 13 children in my family, I was the only one interested in catering and I used to cook with my mum. I even won a cooking competition for the school. When I left, I took a catering course at college. After I qualified I took a job running a pub and I've also cooked in many restaurants.

Now I work for a catering company that provides meals for local schools. I'm the kitchen supervisor at a big junior school. All the staff working for the catering company are trained in health and safety, food hygiene, and the safe use of cleaning substances. Everyone goes on a training course every 2 years.

Our jobs have changed recently. We used to reheat ready meals but now we prepare fresh food ourselves. I get into work at 7.30 a.m. and chop up all the vegetables for the day. I order food for the following week – I have to keep to a tight budget. I check we have everything we need for lunch. Then I help prepare the food, supervising the kitchen staff closely. By 11.45 all the food is in the oven and we have a tea break. After lunch we wash up, and we're finished by 2.30 p.m.

Cooking fresh food is harder work, but the children love the new menus. The biggest reward is when children come up to me saying, "Nuala, that was the best meal I've ever eaten!"

The work environment

Working environments in catering vary greatly. If you're cooking, chances are you will be in a hot, busy, steamy, and noisy kitchen. At peak times, people will be working under pressure, so you need to keep your cool. Kitchens are dangerous places, with all the hot ovens and heavy and sharp equipment. Being aware of safety is crucial. On the positive side, there is often a great team spirit and you can have a good laugh.

From eight till late

In many cases, you will be on the job for such long hours that your working life becomes part of your lifestyle. A catering job can be very sociable. You will probably make friends among your co-workers – around a third of employees in hotels and restaurants are under 24! And you will get to know your regular customers.

above: *In a busy kitchen in a large restaurant, the pressure can get intense.*

Daily routines vary according to the job you are doing. If you are preparing school dinners, your shift could be from 9.45 a.m. to 2 p.m. But if you are working a double-shift in a restaurant, you could be on the job from 8.30 a.m. until midnight, with a couple of hours off mid-afternoon.

Jane, a trainee chef, describes her mid-week double-shift in a small restaurant: "I start work at 8.30 or 9 a.m., depending on when the first delivery arrives. Usually my boss leaves me a list of things to do. I always go through the fridges to check everything is ready for breakfast and turn the ovens on. I sign in the deliveries for the restaurant and the bar.

"Around mid-morning, after I've done the breakfasts, another chef comes in and we do the lunches. I have a 2-hour break from 3 until 5 p.m. I find it is better not to relax too much, though! Then I'm back on for the dinner shift. If it's quiet, we can start cleaning down at about 9 p.m. and close up around 11 p.m."

Benefits of shift work

For most catering jobs you will need to be flexible – starting early, finishing late, and working weekends and bank holidays. You will get days off during the week. There are some benefits to this lifestyle to consider when you decide what job to do. For example, you can be free for shopping and sport while most other people are at work.

CUSTOMER IS KING

If you're out on the floor serving in a restaurant or café, it may be noisy and crowded. You always have to be aware of customers' needs. Mostly they will be polite, but if occasionally they are rude, you will need to remain calm.

Getting into catering

To do well in catering, you should have a real passion for food. Try out different styles of cooking to challenge your taste buds. If possible, visit an inexpensive local restaurant where tasty, fresh food is cooked.

Get your apron on!

Why not practise your cooking skills at home? Start with simple food, such as pasta dishes. Don't be afraid to try out your own ideas and introduce different flavours, including herbs and spices. You will be able to adapt your recipes to suit a fancy restaurant or an ordinary café. The basic skills are the same.

Background education

A good general education is important. It will be useful to have several GCSEs (A–E)/S-grades (1–5), including Maths, English, and ICT. Some GCSEs/S-grades are related to catering. In Home Economics courses, you will learn about health and nutrition as well as food choices and preparation. Applied Health and Social Care includes nutrition and diet too. Food technology is part of the Design and Technology course and involves studying the food industry.

below: *You can practise your cooking skills at home, and help out at the same time!*

Bringing home the bacon

The catering industry is known for low pay rates. It is true that many of the less skilled jobs are poorly paid. But in the commercial sector, you will receive tips from customers on top of your wages. If you work your way up and gain qualifications, the pay improves. Managers can earn good salaries. People will always need to eat so you should always have work!

CASE STUDY

Jane McKenna is a catering student.

I've been working part-time in restaurants since I was 13. At 19, I began doing kitchen work full-time. Then I worked for a chef in a pub. He suggested that I start training to get properly qualified. I didn't want to study full-time so I decided to take a part-time course, which means I can earn a living at the same time. I'm doing a work-based learning course at City College, Brighton, working towards Food Preparation NVQ Level 2. I go to college one day a week and have a work placement at a small restaurant.

I work with four other chefs. I started in the kitchen on the cold side, preparing starters and desserts. Now I'm on the hot side, learning to use the grill to prepare steaks and other meat dishes. I can do the breakfasts on my own now. I found it daunting at first, especially because I'm the only female chef. But I'm picking up the job really quickly. Once I've finished this course, I may take a Level 3 Larder and Main Kitchen course. Then I would like to get a catering job that allows me to go off and see the world.

Chapter 2

In the kitchen

Kitchens are busy places! Apart from the cooking work, there are many jobs in food preparation. About half of all catering staff work as kitchen assistants.

Kitchen assistant

In this job, you learn to carry out basic food preparation tasks to help the chefs and make sure they have everything they need. You learn how to prepare food in a clean and safe environment and how to store food safely to prevent it from spoiling. Very importantly, you learn how to avoid food poisoning. An assistant's job includes helping with the washing up and making sure the equipment, surfaces, walls, and floor are kept spotlessly clean.

You have to be prepared to do quite a lot of routine jobs. There may well be some heavy lifting work when you unload deliveries from suppliers and organize the storeroom. In a small outlet, you may be serving customers as well as keeping the kitchen clean and tidy. All this work provides a good training for becoming a chef.

below: *Kitchen assistants help to keep busy kitchens running smoothly, hygienically, and safely.*

right: *This diagram shows the kitchen chain of command.*

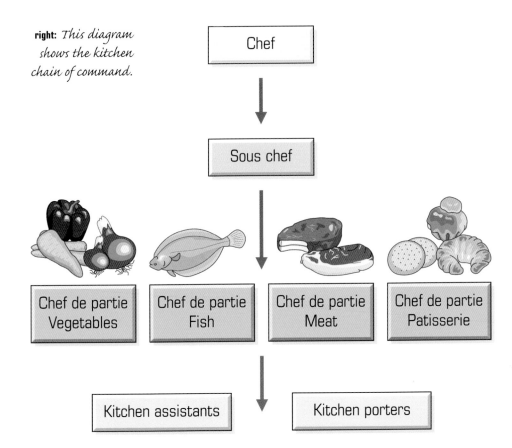

Chef

↓

Sous chef

↓

| Chef de partie Vegetables | Chef de partie Fish | Chef de partie Meat | Chef de partie Patisserie |

↓

Kitchen assistants ↓ Kitchen porters

Kitchen porter

Kitchen porters do some of the same jobs as assistants, keeping the kitchen clean and safe. They are responsible for doing the washing up and mopping the floors at the end of the shift. Special anti-bacterial cleaning products are used to keep the workplace free from germs. Porters help unload deliveries and take out the rubbish. They may help prepare food too. To do this job, you need to be fit and strong to lift heavy equipment and utensils.

Get ahead!

Find out about the variety of kitchen jobs available in your area. There are usually plenty of jobs because there is a high **turnover** in the industry. Many people take on this kind of work as a temporary job while they are studying or to get experience while they are training. They then move on, leaving a vacancy. Check out Springboard UK at: www.springboarduk.org.uk/careers and look in the job search box on the right.

Head chef

The head chef is in overall charge of the kitchen. If you are working for a large company or chain, you will cook according to a fixed standard. You produce food to particular recipes, with little scope for variation. Everything is already decided – the size, weight, and colour of the dish, and how it is presented on the plate. The tasks of managing the budget, buying supplies, and planning menus may be carried out at head office.

At independent establishments, the head chef can be more creative. As Indian restaurant owner Mohammed says: "I experiment a lot and create my own dishes. We use only fresh ingredients. All our spices are bought fresh, and we grind them and mix them ourselves. It's like a chemist's job!"

below: *Chefs wear a fresh white outfit every day, including a clean hat.*

Multiple roles

Head chefs have many roles as well as being in charge of cooking. They often plan the menus, order the produce and other supplies, arrange deliveries, and do the **stock taking**.

Chefs organize every aspect of running the kitchen, from recruiting the staff to arranging the bin collections. They make sure the kitchen is kept clean and sparkling. A good chef knows about how the whole restaurant runs – not just the kitchen – and is aware of what happens to the food once it leaves the kitchen.

CASE STUDY

Vanessa Nickerson is a chef.

I started my career as a kitchen porter, preparing vegetables and washing pots. After a year I started training to be a **sous chef** *as an* **apprentice** *in a small city restaurant. At the same time I attended college to get my Basic Food and Hygiene and Health and Safety Certificates. I was a sous chef for a few years before I eventually worked my way up to the position of head chef.*

It's a hard job. You have to be able to work well as part of a team because you are often in a small, hot space for 14 hours or more a day. You need to be a good organizer and **multi-tasker***, and have the ability to think ahead. When you are busy and under pressure, you have to be able to keep your cool,* **delegate** *well, and be prepared to help out with whatever needs doing – even if it means cleaning out the bottom of a mucky fridge.*

It's tough at first. You need to be able to put your head down, take in information and criticism, and be willing to learn. It is a hard job, but when you have a real passion for food and are working with a friendly bunch, you will find that it can be a very rewarding and fun job.

The butcher, the baker ... and the confectioner

You might be interested in one of these specialist trades to do with preparing food.

Meat to eat

Butchers work in shops and supermarkets. They cut, bone, and trim meat. Butchers buy and order stock and may produce their own meat-based products, including sausages, burgers, and pies. Depending on where you live, there may be demand for **kosher** meat for Jewish customers, **halal** meat for Muslims, or organic meat. To produce kosher or halal meat, the animal has to be slaughtered and the meat prepared in a special way. Organic meat comes from animals that have been allowed to live and feed naturally and have not been given any medicines to make them grow faster.

In addition to creating meat products, you will also serve customers and may offer them advice on how to cook their meat. You will need to be fit to carry large joints of meat and have good awareness of workplace hygiene. The job involves contact with raw meat, so if you have allergies or skin conditions, it may not suit you.

right: Bakers have to use precise recipes to get a delicious result every time.

Earning your crust

Bakers produce a wide range of goods, from delicious crusty bread to tasty pies and celebration cakes. Job opportunities include working at a large **plant bakery**, an in-store supermarket bakery or a small craft bakery. If you work at a plant bakery, you will use machinery to produce large quantities of bread for supermarkets. At an in-store bakery you will also use machinery. At craft bakeries, which are smaller, you will make a wider variety of bread and cakes for specialist shops. You will work mostly by hand, which can be quite creative. Warning: bakers start work very early in the morning! If your job is in a plant bakery, you will do shifts, which can involve evening and night-time work.

Sweet treats

You are sure to be popular if you go into chocolate making! Many people become chocolatiers after working in related areas, such as cake decorating. Chocolatiers use machines to melt the chocolate and moulds to produce the shapes, but they decorate the chocolates by hand. As well as being a careful worker, you will need patience to master the decorating skills, which include brushwork to paint on details and piping to create designs.

Get ahead!

There is a national shortage of staff in the bakery, confectionery, and butchery industries, and they are all keen to recruit young people. In particular there is a lack of skilled workers, so if you're willing to train, you will improve your career potential. See pages 22–23 and, for meat training, look at these websites – www.meattraining.org.uk (England and Wales); www.foodtraining.net (Scotland).

below: *Chocolatiers add the finishing touches by hand.*

Cut out for kitchen work?

So what kind of person do you need to be to work in a kitchen? It will vary to an extent, depending on whether you are working in a little tea shop in a sleepy village or the kitchen of a top-notch city restaurant.

In general, you will need to be outgoing, friendly, and **tactful**. You will be happy to work long hours, including evenings and weekends. You won't mind working split shifts – long shifts with a break in the middle. Kitchen work is tiring, and you will need to be able to cope when things get hectic. Even though working in a kitchen can be stressful, if you have a good team, you will have a lot of fun.

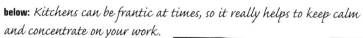

below: *Kitchens can be frantic at times, so it really helps to keep calm and concentrate on your work.*

Qualified for a hot job?

Obviously, you will need to love food and ideally have some knowledge of cooking already. It is useful to have an awareness of food hygiene and safety. It will be helpful to get several GCSE/S-grades, including English. Science and Maths are useful for measuring ingredients, calculating cooking times, and understanding cooking temperatures. Design and Technology, which includes food technology, is relevant too.

Entry-level qualifications

You can get a job as a kitchen assistant and porter and do some training to help you work your way up to a better job. For example, kitchen assistants can work towards **National Vocational Qualification** (NVQ) **or Scottish Vocational Qualification** (SVQ) Level 1 in Preparing and Serving Food and Levels 1 and 2 in Food Preparation and Cooking. Kitchen porters can take NVQ/SVQ Level 1 in Kitchen Portering. See Chapter 4 for more details about training.

Specialist areas

For butchers, bakers, and confectioners, special courses are available, although much of your learning will be on the job. You can have training through an **apprenticeship** to learn to be a baker. You will work towards Bakery NVQ/SVQs Levels 1–3. For plant bakery work, the most relevant NVQ/SVQs are Food and Drink Manufacturing Operations Levels 1–3. Trainee butchers can work towards NVQ/SVQ Levels 2 and 3 in Meat and Poultry Processing. The Meat Training Council provides its own vocational qualifications. If you want to be a chocolatier, you could go for NVQ/SVQ Level 3 in **Patisserie** and Confectionery.

SLIPS AND TRIPS

Kitchens can be dangerous places, so there are strict regulations concerning health and safety in the workplace. The biggest hazard is falling over on a wet floor, followed by injuries from lifting heavy objects and from handling sharp objects. Find out more about health and safety in catering at: www.hse.gov.uk/catering/

Chapter 3

Caring for customers

If you can't stand the heat... get out of the kitchen! There are many jobs that involve serving customers rather than preparing food. They vary from working behind a self-service counter in a local café to being a highly skilled **silver-service waiter** or waitress in a luxury hotel.

At your service

As a waiter or waitress, you will welcome customers, take orders, serve food, and clean and prepare tables. It is hard work, and you will be on your feet the whole time. But the working environment in the dining area is not as hot and steamy as in the kitchen. You have a big responsibility to care for customers, because the quality of the service can be just as important as the food. In some places, counter-service assistants serve the food from a hatch rather than waiting on tables.

Silver-service waiters in formal restaurants serve the meal in a particular way, for example bringing the main part of the meal separately from the side dishes. Senior waiters advise diners on the menu as well as serving food.

above: *For people having a meal in a restaurant, the service is just as important as the food.*

You will need to be clean and smart to do this job and have high standards of personal hygiene. Your employer will usually provide you with a uniform. In most jobs you will work shifts, including evening, weekend, and bank holiday work.

David Herranz is a waiter.

I've always loved cooking as a hobby. Back in Spain, I worked in my family's restaurant. I came to the UK and got a job as a waiter in a noodle bar. I've had all my training on the job. I work around 35 hours a week in 6- or 7-hour shifts. I'm also studying English at college.

I enjoy the contact with people and practising the language. Most people are great but occasionally customers can be rude, which is quite upsetting. You just have to carry on with the job.

I'd recommend working as a waiter while you're studying. The shifts are flexible and you will get valuable work experience for a career in catering.

FINE WINE

A sommelier is a wine waiter or waitress who has specialist knowledge of wines. As a sommelier, you buy wine for the pub or restaurant and advise customers about the wines on the drinks list. To get this job, it is useful to have experience of bar or restaurant work as well as knowing about food and wine. An NVQ/SVQ in Catering and Hospitality is helpful too. Other relevant qualifications are NVQ/SVQs Levels 1 and 2 in Food and Drink Service. You will need a good palette – the ability to taste the difference in wines. As part of the job, you will go to wine tastings to try out new products.

right: *Advising customers which wine is best with which food is a skilled job.*

Pulling the pints

Bar staff work in **licensed premises** including pubs, clubs, wine bars, and hotels, and also in sports, leisure, and holiday centres. As a bar worker, you will serve drinks, clear tables, and wash glasses. Many pubs serve food, so you may learn to cook and serve food as well as drinks. Nowadays, drinking wine is popular, so it helps if you know what to recommend. Being friendly and welcoming is vital in this job.

Bars get noisy and crowded. Your working hours will be long and late, especially if you work in a night-club. You will be clearing up well after the clubbers are tucked up in bed. On the positive side, it can be a sociable environment, working with other young people.

It is worth knowing that in England and Wales, if you are under 18 you are only allowed to work in a pub if you are on an apprenticeship scheme.

CASE STUDY

Ian Sillett is a licensee.

I've worked in pubs since I turned 18, and I'm also a musician. When I was at university, I worked in a student pub where I ran the karaoke and open-mic sessions. Now I work in a local pub. A good mix of people of all ages drink here, including students, locals, and even the former city mayor! We have lots of live music.

During the week we're open until midnight, but we usually close at 11 p.m. because it's quiet by then. On weekends we stay open until 1 a.m. If there's a bank holiday coming up, we can get special permission from the local **magistrate** *to stay open even later.*

I love the social side of the job. To work in a bar you have to get on well with all sorts of people. We get some real characters in here, and you need to make an effort to be friendly to them, even though it tests your patience at times! At Christmas we have a benefit gig and use the money to hold a party for local children. We also raise money for charity. My pub is a major focus of the community.

above: *Working in a bar can be a sociable job.*

LEGAL CHANGES

In 2005, changes in the law took place that affected licensed premises. Before, they had to close at 11 p.m. between Monday and Saturday. Now, the licensee can apply for a license to remain open for longer hours. This means bar workers often work later at night, especially at weekends. If you are considering bar work, note that every bar will have its own opening hours. In 2006, a law was introduced to ban smoking in public places from 2007. Bar workers will no longer have to work in a smoky atmosphere.

Fast on your feet?

Every town and city in the UK has fast-food outlets, from international burger and pizza chains to family-run take-away restaurants selling fish and chips, Indian, Chinese or Middle-Eastern dishes.

Cutting the mustard

Many young people work in the fast-food industry. It is a very flexible industry, with great opportunities to work part-time while you are studying. Pay is usually based on an hourly rate. If you are a fast-food worker you will probably have to cook as well as serve food. You take it in turns to serve, cook, or work on the till. In many fast-food restaurants, there is little real cooking to be done. The ready-cooked meals arrive at the restaurant frozen or freeze-dried and just have to be reheated.

If you are working on the till in a drive-through restaurant, you will wear a headset and take customers' orders through an intercom system. You need to work quickly and accurately to process their orders.

above: *Fast-food workers serve huge numbers of people during busy times.*

All fast-food jobs involve working quickly at busy times. You may have to serve at least one customer per minute! There are busy times throughout the day. You may be rushed off your feet at lunchtime in particular. On weekdays, school children may fill up your restaurant after 4 p.m. and they will come with their families at the weekend. Even late at night, fast-food restaurants are full of people grabbing something to eat on the way home from an evening out.

Before you start, you will get training at your workplace. You will learn how to prepare the food and use the kitchen equipment and the till. You will find out about health and safety rules too. Customer service forms a crucial part of the training.

CASE STUDY

Jenny Matthews is a crew member at a fast-food chain.

I've been working for the same fast-food chain for nearly 3 years. I needed an easy and decently paid holiday job while I was at university. Being a crew member fitted in well with my studies. The hours are flexible – you can work different hours each week. At first I trained at a drive-through restaurant, where I learnt how to use the till and take orders politely and quickly. I was also trained in health and safety and how to prepare the food correctly. All my training has been on the job. Now I'm experienced, my wages are quite good.

A typical shift is 7 hours. I get in, wash carefully, and check my uniform is smart. Then I'm on my feet all day, serving customers. I get a 45-minute break during the shift.

There are good points about the job. It's not stressful – I don't go home worrying about work. The other crew members are a good bunch. There's a great mix of people from many different countries, and we all get on really well. Sometimes we get together outside work. On the other hand, I do realize there are problems with fast food. It's fine to eat it now and again, but I am concerned about the health of people who come here a lot.

Do you fit the bill?

If you are going to be serving people, it goes without saying that you should be good at communicating with all kinds of customers – including the awkward type! If you are considering working in a fast-food restaurant, you need to get on well with children, as they are important customers. For all jobs you will need to be fit, because you will be on your feet most of the time. You will often have to work at speed and under pressure. Having a good memory for faces is a bonus, as customers appreciate it if you recognize them.

In pubs and clubs you will need to be alert in case any trouble develops. On occasions, some people may become aggressive when they have had too many drinks or if they can't get served quickly. You will need to be able to stay calm.

below: *Bar staff in busy clubs have to work quickly and stay calm.*

School subjects

As for most jobs, several GCSE/S-grades will stand you in good stead. Good standards of numeracy and literacy are required for being a waiter/waitress, so Maths and English will help. Counter service assistants need good mental arithmetic for giving the correct change. If you can speak any foreign languages, this is definitely a point in your favour. To enter some jobs – to be a sommelier, for example – employers expect good GCSE/S-grades.

Training on the job

It is possible to get a job as a waiter/waitress, fast-food worker or barperson without experience or qualifications. You will be trained on the job, and there are qualifications you can gain. Some establishments run their own training schemes through which you will get health and safety training, and fire training – especially in pubs and clubs.

While on the job, you can work towards qualifications such as NVQ/SVQs in Catering and Hospitality (see page 38). Fast-food workers can take NVQ/SVQ Hospitality Quick Service Level 2. The bar industry has its own qualifications, organized through the British Institute of Innkeeping. Bar staff work towards the Professional Barperson's Qualification.

HOSPITALITY

A related area to catering is the hospitality industry – looking after visitors to hotels and guesthouses. It is possible to move into hotel work with catering experience. Some jobs involve working directly with customers, such as the receptionist, the concierge (who provides information to clients), and the manager. Other jobs involve keeping the hotel clean, tidy, and in good repair – the housekeeper and caretaker take charge of these tasks. And, of course, large hotels will have a restaurant and bar. Check out Connexions Direct at: www.connexions-direct.com. In the Careers section, there are resources you can download including the Working in... series. No. 468 is about Catering and Hospitality.

Chapter 4

A foot in the door

When you are in Year 10 or 11, you will be able to get a **work experience placement**, organized by your school. It is usually for 2 weeks in England and Wales, and for 1 week in Scotland.

Work experience

Work experience can help you see the relevance of what you are learning in school to a job you might do in the future.

If you choose to do work experience in catering, bear in mind that job titles don't tell you very much. The tasks and level of responsibility depend on the kind of establishment, its size, and the type of services it provides. So it is worth finding out about the workplace before you start. If your local college runs a catering course, you may be able to do work experience in the kitchen. This should prove less hectic than a professional kitchen!

Before you start your placement, the school will arrange a health and safety inspection of the workplace. And health and safety will be the main subject of your preparation sessions at school. One aspect of this is dressing appropriately for the job. Check what you will need to wear and make sure you are spotlessly clean and tidy.

On the placement, you will probably help another worker to do his or her job or you may be given your own tasks. However tired you are at the end of the day, do not forget to write down the day's activities in your diary and log book.

Get ahead!

After your work experience placement, you will talk about your experiences in class and write up your log book or diary for assessment. You could make notes on the following to help you:
◎ Good points about the placement
◎ Any problems and what you learnt from them
◎ Training and help you received on the job
◎ Skills you used
◎ Your opinions of the work and whether your experience has helped you decide what job you would like to do.

above: *Doing work experience in a catering company can start your career rolling.*

CASE STUDY

Alan Wark, a Year 10 student, describes his work experience placement.

I'd like to be a chef so I decided to do work experience in a kitchen. My work placement was at a nursing home. On the first day I arrived, I was a bag of nerves. I didn't know what to expect.

When I entered the kitchen, it looked exactly like my school canteen. It was large and very clean, and all the fittings were stainless steel. The chef showed me the storeroom. We had a delivery of supplies, and I put them away and tidied the storeroom. I helped chop the vegetables with a special cutter and used a food mixer to prepare sauces for lunch. I also helped clear the tables and do the washing-up after lunch.

Once I knew what I needed to do I really enjoyed myself and I learnt a lot. I thought all the staff would look down on me and get me to do all of the boring jobs, but they were very nice and treated me like the others.

above: *It is important to be very attentive to instructions when you start a job.*

Talk to the bosses

If you're going for a job in catering, how can you impress the boss at your interview?

Managers in this industry often look more at the experience and personality of applicants than at their qualifications. Qualifications have greater importance at higher levels, though. Employers want you to be able to work well with the other staff and the customers. Excellent communication skills are vital. You will need to understand the customers' needs and use your initiative to solve any problems. Bosses like you to be eager to learn and able to follow instructions.

As well as having the right personality, good basic numeracy and literacy skills are important. You will have an advantage if you already have job-specific skills. If you want to do kitchen work, it will help if you are already a keen budding cook. You may already have gained useful skills from part-time jobs or from your home cooking experiences.

Keir Bottrill is a catering supervisor.

*I work for a company that organizes the catering for a large private school. I'm in charge of the dining room and the servery (the counter where we serve meals). We cater for 1,200 students and staff on a daily basis and we also organize the food and drink for big functions such as weddings and conferences. I've got 15 people working under me and I have to make sure they do their jobs properly. If a problem crops up, I have to solve it – fast. Perhaps a member of staff falls sick or there is a problem with the timing of the dinner. If you're good at **troubleshooting**, you're good at catering! It's hard work and it can be stressful, but I love the job. A big advantage is getting paid school holidays, so I can do lots of travelling.*

When I'm recruiting, personality is very important. I need enthusiastic staff who will be loyal to the company. Good references are vital – I ask for written references or I phone up the referees. Previous experience is necessary too. If I'm employing a chef, the applicant must have City and Guilds 7061 and 7062 and a Food Hygiene Certificate.

My advice to students is to go for the best grades you can at school. Then it will be easier to progress at work and take further courses. The lower-level jobs in catering aren't very well paid. Aim for a career in management because there are exciting jobs available and you will earn a good salary.

Planning your career

There are different ways to get into the catering industry. You can get a job, work while training, or study first before taking the plunge.

above: *These catering college students are working in the kitchen with their tutor.*

Get a job

If you want to start working at 16, it will be ideal to have GCSEs (A–C) or S-grades (1–3). Key subjects are English, Maths, and ICT. Foreign languages are also helpful. It is quite easy to get your first job at a junior level. Most people in the industry start at the bottom and work their way up. At first, you will have to be prepared to do anything. In your first job in a kitchen, you will probably be washing pots and pans and clearing up.

Make sure that your employer offers training. Most will provide job-specific training to teach you how to do your job properly. Employers should give you health and safety training as required by the law.

Become an apprentice

If you are aged 16 to 24, you can start an apprenticeship (England and Wales) or Skillseekers course (Scotland). This is a highly recommended way to enter the industry. You can begin an apprenticeship if you are just starting out or have been in the industry for a while. You can get trained, gain experience and qualifications, and earn a wage, all at the same time! You will work most days and probably attend college one day a week. Most of your training is on the job, with support from your college tutors.

It generally takes one or two years to complete an apprenticeship. It usually leads to NVQ/SVQ Levels 1 and 2 and a **technical certificate** (see pages 38–39). The course is funded by the government, so you won't have to pay a penny. Students are often tempted to leave their apprenticeship before they finish because they have achieved their first NVQ/SVQ and been offered a better job. But it is worth staying the course. The qualifications will help you progress in your career.

CASE STUDY

James Mason is a catering apprentice.

At school, I got 6 GCSEs, grades C–F. I've always loved cooking and I used to have a part-time job as a weekend chef. Now I'm on a 13-month apprenticeship in Food Preparation and Cooking, leading to NVQ Levels 1 and 2. I attend college one day a week. The rest of the time I work as a chef in a private nursing home. We cook a variety of food, from curry to roast dinner. I love food! My favourite dish is fillet steak, and I enjoy making cakes and pastries. After this course, I plan to do NVQ Level 3 in Patisserie. My aim is to get a job as a chef on a cruise ship.

left: *Catering students may work as waiters and waitresses while they are training.*

Studying for qualifications

At 16, you can study at college full or part-time for various qualifications. These are subject to change, so check carefully what is available.

NVQ/SVQs

A National Vocational Qualification (NVQ) or Scottish Vocational Qualification (SVQ) is a work-related award. It proves that you know how to do your job. You can take NVQ/SVQs if you are working full or part-time. Generally, you will go to college one day a week. At work, you complete many of the tasks that you need to do to achieve your qualification. There are five levels of NVQ/SVQs. After a 2-year apprenticeship, you will probably achieve Level 2 and a technical certificate. Catering NVQs include Food and Drink Service, Preparing and Serving Food, and Hospitality and Catering.

GCSEs and A Levels

There are full-time courses in vocational subjects that introduce you to a sector of work and prepare you for further vocational study or a job. A GCSE in a vocational subject is equivalent to two ordinary GCSEs. From 2009, you will able to take a GCSE in Hospitality and Catering. There is a Vocational A-level in the same subject and one in Hospitality Management. Alternatively, you could take regular A-levels/Highers.

National Award/Certificate/Diploma

The **National Award**, **National Certificate**, and **National Diploma** courses each lead to a vocational qualification. You can take them part-time while working or full-time before going into the industry. Examples of catering courses are the **BTEC** National Award in Hospitality and Catering and the BTEC National Award in Food Science and Manufacturing Technology. To get on to these courses, you will need four GCSEs (A–C) or S-grades (1–3) or equivalent.

Specialized diplomas

Available from 2008, these new qualifications for 14 to 19-year-olds will help you master essential skills in maths, English, ICT and other skills, and learn to apply them in work situations. There are three levels. A **diploma** in Hospitality and Catering will be available from 2009.

Jane, who is studying Food Preparation, explains how you work towards an NVQ: "At college, we spend the morning in the kitchen with our tutor, preparing two or three dishes. In the afternoon we go through the theory of what we've done in the kitchen. Also, if there are things we don't understand at work, we can ask questions. We all have a folder where we tick off the tasks we've done at college and in our work placement. My head chef at work helps me to cook dishes that I have to do to tick the boxes in my folder. The work in our folder will later be assessed. Our tutor also assesses us at the workplace."

above: *Catering students watch professional chefs give a cooking demonstration.*

Further study options

Large numbers of people in the catering industry have not achieved high-level qualifications. For example, only 10 per cent of restaurant staff and 14 per cent of staff in pubs, bars, and nightclubs have achieved NVQ Level 4. If you are well qualified, you should have no problem finding a good job.

Advanced apprenticeships

These are for people aged 16 to 24 who already have work experience and have reached NVQ/SVQ Level 2. You will also need to have at least four GCSEs (A–C) or S-grades (1–3). If you enter this scheme, you will work full-time, with the aim of becoming a supervisor or junior manager. It will take you at least 2 years to qualify and you will achieve at least NVQ/SVQ Level 3 and a technical certificate.

Professional qualifications

Most professions have their own training schemes with a range of qualifications you can take. For example, if you want to qualify in pub management, you can take a course with the British Institute of Innkeeping. The Academy of Culinary Arts runs specialized chefs' courses. The Bakery Training Council is the national training organization for the bakery industry. The Hotel and Catering International Management Association runs training programmes relevant to the hospitality, leisure, and tourism industries.

HNC/HND

There are some more options for over-18s. **Higher National Certificates** (HNCs) and **Higher National Diplomas** (HNDs) are like degrees but in vocational subjects. You can take an HNC over 1 year full-time or 2 years part-time. Catering subjects include Professional Cookery and Professional Patisserie. An HND usually takes 2 years full-time. Subjects include Food Science and Technology, the Food Industry, and Hotel, Catering and Institutional Management. You will need at least four GCSEs/S-grades and one A-level/Advanced Higher or equivalent (such as NVQ/SVQ Level 3) to get on to an HNC or HND course.

Degrees

Another option is to take a **foundation degree** at a Further Education (FE) college. There are no set entry requirements. Or you could take a university degree in a subject such as Hospitality Management or Hotel and Catering Management. To get in, you will need at least two A-levels/Advanced Highers, or a vocational A-level. With an HNC/HND or a degree, you can kick-start a career in catering management.

Study options – at a glance

Under 16 *
GCSEs/S-grades
Vocational GCSEs/S-grades

At 16
Apprenticeship/Skillseekers, leading to NVQ/SVQ Level 2 and Technical Certificate NVQ/SVQs while on the job
Vocational A-level/Higher
Regular A-levels/Highers
National Award/Certificate/Diploma
Specialized Diploma
Advanced Apprenticeship leading to NVQ/SVQ Level 3 or 4 and Technical Certificate

At 18
Higher National Certificate
Higher National Diploma
Foundation Degree
Degree

For experienced catering workers
Professional qualifications

* These qualifications can be taken when you're older

Get ahead!

If you reach NVQ/SVQ Level 3, you will have good job opportunities. For example, with an NVQ/SVQ in Food Preparation and Cooking, you could get a job as junior chef and work your way up to head chef. With an Advanced Craft Drink Service qualification, you could go into bar or restaurant management. An Advanced Craft Food Service NVQ/SVQ could help land you a job as a head waiter/waitress or assistant restaurant manager.

right: *Gaining qualifications gives you pride as well as greater job opportunities.*

Chapter 5

Top jobs

Could you cater for varying numbers of people with minimum waste? Could you make sure you have enough staff during busy periods and not too many standing idle when things are quiet? With some experience, patience, and hard work, it is possible to reach a managerial position in the catering industry. You need to be a good organizer and know how to manage staff. When the staff are frantic, you will have to roll up your sleeves and help out.

below: *Restaurant managers must ensure that all supplies are up-to-date and correctly stored.*

Restaurant manager

A manager's responsibilities vary greatly, depending on the kind of establishment. You could be managing a hotel or independent restaurant or a fast-food joint. If you work for a chain, you may not need to order food and plan menus, as this is probably done at head office. But you may be allowed some choice over the food you serve as long as you keep to the budget and price range for the meals. As well as ensuring high-quality food is prepared, you will be in charge of ordering stock, ensuring all the kitchen machinery works, and keeping to a strict budget. Your responsibilities will also include recruiting and training staff, organizing the rota, and keeping everyone motivated to do the job well. As the manager, you will have contact with the customers, welcoming them and making sure they enjoy their meal.

Kitchen supervisor

Every kitchen has supervisors, who are in charge of their own section. All supervisors are trained chefs de partie (section chefs). They divide up the tasks among their team and deal with health and safety matters and any problems. Most supervisors start off as kitchen assistants or trainee chefs and progress by gaining qualifications and experience.

FAST MOVERS

The fast-food industry is a competitive business, with lots of money to be made. The industry is full of young people, and it can be relatively easy to get promoted to supervisor level. You will have to work your way up, though. Starting as a fast-food service assistant, you will learn to work in all sections – counter, till, and kitchen. If you do well, you can progress to managing a small team through to managing the entire shift. You could train further to become manager of the restaurant. Some people enter the industry at managerial level with a degree or HND in Catering, Business Studies or even with an arts degree. But they all have to learn how to cook and serve as part of their training.

Catering manager

There are some catering jobs where you won't be hands-on in the kitchen or dealing directly with customers. You will be supervising other people who do these jobs.

Many workplaces, schools, hospitals, and transport systems have a contract with a catering company to provide their food and drink. This is called contract catering. The company employs a catering manager. In this job, you will oversee the catering at all the sites you manage. You will visit them regularly to keep a check on health and safety, food quality, the staff, and the budget. Part of your job will be marketing – finding new customers to expand the business. You will need to understand the food industry to judge how your company can succeed. You will also be involved in overseeing staff training.

above: *This catering manager needs good communication skills to give instructions to students at a catering college.*

As catering manager, you have responsibility for the food the company serves up. You plan the menus and work out the costs, which include all kitchen supplies and wages for the staff. You make deals with suppliers to buy ingredients in bulk. As your company is producing food on a big scale, large amounts of machinery are used. You need to keep up to date with changes in technology so you know when to buy new equipment.

Your hours are usually more regular than in other parts of the industry. You tend to work weekdays only, rather than shifts.

School meals organizer

As school meals organizer for a catering company, you could be arranging the delivery of ready-cooked meals to some schools in the area and checking cooking and hygiene standards where food is cooked on-site. You will check the staff are making the food properly. As schools are always trying to improve the dinners they provide, you will be talking to teachers, school governors, and parents. You will probably discuss how you can cut down on sugar and salt in the menus and encourage children to eat fresh fruit. You will make sure you get feedback from your young customers to see if they are enjoying their dinners. But you know you can't give them pizza every day, even if that is what they would like!

CASE STUDY

John Cadien is a catering manager.

I've achieved my ambition to be a catering manager, even though I'm a wheelchair user. After a catering course, I took a 3-year catering management course at Henley College, Coventry. Through my work experience placement and studies, I gained technical and interpersonal skills. Then I took a job as catering manager at a centre for students with disabilities. I successfully developed a strategy to supply food to commercial outlets and earn money for the centre. My latest goal is to set up a community catering business to train disabled people for secure jobs in catering.

Being your own boss

With plenty of experience under your belt, there are plenty of opportunities for self-employment in catering.

Pub life

About half of the pubs in Britain are owned by pub companies. A pub manager works for the company that owns the pub and is paid a salary. Pub managers often receive free accommodation. Nearly a third of pubs are independent, called free houses. The owners have bought the pub outright and are not linked to a particular brewery. The rest are owned by breweries. They are run by self-employed publicans, who pay rent to the brewery. Each pub must have a licensee, who makes sure everyone keeps to the laws on alcohol sales.

Being a licensee is a way of life, as there always has to be a licensee on the premises during opening hours. You order stock, organize the finances, and manage the staff. It is important to have detailed knowledge of licensing laws, entertainment trends, and to know your customers. You set up the pub before the staff arrive, making sure everything is ready and that the tills are set up. You are around to change beer barrels and deal with any difficult situations among the pubgoers. Licensee Ian Sillett (see page 26) says: "The work is very full on and it is exhausting. You live above the pub all the time and it feels like all the customers and staff are in your front room. But I love the sociable lifestyle."

Restaurants

Experienced chefs may open up their own independent restaurant. As the owner, you are responsible for recruiting and training staff, ordering supplies, and managing the budget. You plan the menus, organize the rota, and help in the kitchen.

Mohammed Asaduzzaman owns an Indian restaurant.

I worked in around 15 restaurants all over the country before opening my own restaurant in 1998. We cook specialities from Goa in southern India, such as Goan vindaloo, with red-hot chillies. I gained qualifications in food preparation and hygiene and learned about cooking through reading books. I also took a course for supervisors to gain managerial skills.

There are some downsides. The hours are unlimited. I work 7 days a week, from early in the morning until late at night. We've had trouble from some customers who have been rude and aggressive towards the waiters. But things have improved recently.

Overall, I love the job. I enjoy the contact with different kinds of people and being part of the community. My restaurant raises funds for charities and I offer free training courses for students who want to learn Indian cooking. I've earned great respect for the work I do.

right: *Owning your own restaurant is a demanding but satisfying job.*

Getting a top job

There is no single route to becoming a manager or supervisor, but you will need relevant experience and qualifications.

People skills

You will need to be hardworking, with lots of stamina. It is important to be patient, good at dealing with customers, well organized, and able to stay calm in a crisis. You will know how to make sure your staff stay motivated. Also, you will be good at handling accounts.

The academic route

Academic requirements vary. You may be taken on as a trainee manager with a good level of education including some GCSEs/ S-grades, especially in English and Maths. A second language may be helpful. Other employers want people with A-levels/Highers, a foundation degree, an HNC/HND or a degree.

above: *Once you have catering experience, you can do management training.*

You can take an HND in subjects such as Hotel and Catering Management or Hospitality Management to learn how to organize people and resources at the workplace. You will be able to choose options that particularly interest you, such as conference and banqueting management. There are degrees with similar titles to HNDs. During your degree course you will learn how to supervise the preparation of food and drink and manage a catering business, and also learn about catering technologies. Again, there is a choice of options to specialize in.

On-the-job training

See pages 38–41 for study options. With NVQ/SVQ Levels 1 and 2 under your belt, you can go on to Levels 3 and 4 in your chosen area to help you get into management. If you would like to be a manager in the drinks trade, you could work towards Level 3 in Licensed Premises Supervision Management and Level 4 in Licensed Premises Management. If you are a junior manager or supervisor with Level 2 qualifications, you could enrol for the **Hotel and Catering International Management Association** (HCIMA) Advanced Certificate in Hospitality Studies or take a foundation degree in Hospitality Management.

Success on the menu

Celebrity TV chef Jamie Oliver, who is worth a staggering £20 million, started out with a **City and Guilds** qualification in Catering and Hotel Management. Famous chef Gary Rhodes also began with a City and Guilds course. He now appears on TV, has written bestselling books, and runs top-rated restaurants. You may not end up a millionaire, but with good qualifications and plenty of experience, a career in catering can be an excellent choice.

KEIR'S ROUTE

Chef Keir Bottrill (see page 35) took City and Guilds Food and Hygiene courses 7061 and 7062 to qualify as a chef. In the first year, he studied cooking – everything from chopping vegetables to making sauces and elaborate desserts. In the second year, he learnt management skills for hotel and catering. His qualifications, along with experience, enabled him to get a job as catering supervisor in a school.

right: *TV chef Gary Rhodes at work in the kitchen.*

Jobs in catering

Airline steward

Baker

Bar manager

Barperson

Butcher

Catering manager

Cellar technician

Chef de partie

Confectioner

Consumer scientist

Counter service assistant

Fast-food manager

Fast-food service assistant

Freelance cook

Head chef

Kitchen assistant

Kitchen porter

Kitchen supervisor

Licensee

Publican

Restaurant manager

Restaurant owner

School lunchtime supervisor

School meals organizer

Sommelier

Sous chef

Vending machine operative

Waiter/waitress

Rough annual earnings

◎ **Airline steward**
Starting salary: £10–12,000
Experienced: £14–18,000
Senior: £22,000

◎ **Baker**
Starting salary: £10–12,000
Experienced: £15,500
Senior: £22,500

◎ **Barperson**
Starting salary: £6,600–9,000
Experienced: £16,200

◎ **Butcher**
Starting salary: £10,000
Experienced: £11–13,000
Manager: £12–17,500

◎ **Catering manager/supervisor**
Junior: £10–18,000
Experienced: £20–27,000
Senior: £40,000

◎ **Chef**
Junior chef: £9–11,000
Chef de partie: £16,000
Sous chef: £16,500–£19,800
Head chef: £19,000–£26,000
or more

◎ **Confectioner**
Starting salary: £10,000
Experienced: £12,000
Supervisor: £20,000

◎ **Fast–food manager**
Trainee: £17,000
Restaurant manager: £32,000

◎ **Fast–food service assistant**
Starting salary: £8,500

◎ **Kitchen assistant**
£7,500–£16,000

◎ **Kitchen porter**
£7,500–£16,000

◎ **Kitchen supervisor**
Trainee: £13,000
Experienced: £23,000
Senior: up to £33,000

◎ **Licensee/pub manager**
Trainee: £14–18,000
Experienced: £25,000

◎ **Restaurant manager/owner**
(Similar to catering manager)

◎ **Sommelier**
Starting salary: £10,000
Experienced: £16,000
Head sommelier: £20,000

◎ **Waiter/waitress**
Starting salary: £8,000 or less
Experienced: £12,000
Head waiter: £17,000

(Figures from Learndirect website and Connexions: *Working in Hospitality and Catering*)

Careers websites

Please note that qualifications and courses are subject to change.

◎ City and Guilds (www.city-and-guilds.co.uk)
   – This website is all about City and Guilds qualifications.

◎ Connexions Direct (www.connexions-direct.com)
   – This website provides information and advice for young people, including training and careers. It includes a link to the Jobs4U careers database.

◎ Learndirect (www.learndirect-advice.co.uk) and Learndirect Scotland (www.learndirectscotland.com/)
   – Go to the "job profiles" for details of many jobs in the catering industry and courses and qualifications.

◎ Modern Apprenticeships, Scotland (www.scottish-enterprise.com/modernapprenticeships)
   – Check out the case studies of people already training.

◎ Need2Know: Learning (www.need2know.co.uk/learning)
   – Information about studying and qualifications.

◎ Qualifications and Curriculum Authority (www.qca.org.uk/14-19)
   – Go to "Qualifications" and click on "Main qualification groups" to find out about NVQs.

◎ Scottish Vocational Qualifications (www.sqa.org.uk)
   – Find out all the latest qualifications information.

◎ The National Council for Work Experience (www.work-experience.org/)
   – Go to "Students and graduates" to search placements.

Get ahead in catering!

◎ Academy of Culinary Arts (www.academyofculinaryarts.org.uk)
   – The Academy of Culinary Arts runs specialized chefs' training for 16 to 19-year-olds.

◎ British Institute of Innkeeping (www.bii.org.uk)
   – The BII is the professional body for the licensed drinks trade.

◎ Hotel and Catering International Management Association (www.hcima.org.uk) – HCIMA runs training programmes relevant to the hospitality, leisure, and tourism industries.

Publications

◎ Boulud, Daniel. *Letters to a Young Chef* (Basic Books, 2003)

◎ Brefere, Lisa M., Karen Eich Drummond and Brad Barnes, *So You Want to Be a Chef? Your Guide to Culinary Careers* (John Wiley, 2005)

◎ Camlee Associates. *Working in Hospitality and Catering* (Connexions, 2004)

◎ Caprione Chemelynski, Carol. *Opportunities in Restaurant Careers* (Contemporary Books, 2004)

◎ Dixon, Beryl. *Getting into Hotels and Catering* (Trotman, 2002)

◎ Dornenburg, Andrew and Karen Page. *Becoming a Chef* (John Wiley, 2003)

◎ Ninemeier, Jack D. and Joe Perdue. *Hospitality Operations: Careers in the World's Greatest Industry* (Prentice Hall, 2004)

◎ Pilgrim, Dee. *Real Life Guides: Catering* (Trotman, 2003)

◎ Sims-Bell, Barbara. *Career Opportunities in the Food and Beverage Industry* (Facts on File, 2001)

apprentice someone working as part of an apprenticeship scheme

apprenticeship training scheme that allows you to work for money, learn, and become qualified at the same time

BTEC Business and Technician Education Council. The qualifications it awards include the Higher National Certificate (HNC) and Higher National Diploma (HND).

City and Guilds leading provider of work-related qualifications in the UK, assessing practical skills that are of use in the workplace

delegate to share out work among your staff

diploma work-related qualification, usually taken after secondary school to provide you with employment skills. There are also post-graduate diplomas.

foundation degree work-related degree. There are no set entry requirements – each college or university has its own requirements.

freelance self-employed rather than working for a company

halal meat from an animal that has been prepared according to Muslim law

Higher National Certificate (HNC) technical qualification that you can take after a National Certificate or after A-levels/Highers

Higher National Diploma (HND) technical qualification that you progress to from an HNC. It usually takes 2 years to achieve.

Hotel and Catering International Management Association (HCIMA) organization that runs training programmes for people in the hospitality industry

initiative the ability to decide and act on your own without waiting for someone else to tell you what to do

kosher meat that has been prepared according to Jewish law

licensed premises place where it is legal for alcohol to be served

licensee person who holds a licence, a legal document allowing them to serve alcoholic drinks on the premises. They have to make sure that everyone on the premises keeps to the law.

magistrate an official who acts as the judge in the lowest courts of law

multitask do lots of different things at the same time

National Award work-related qualification that is equivalent to one A-level

National Certificate work-related qualification that is equivalent to two A-levels

National Diploma work-related qualification that is equivalent to three A-levels

National Vocational Qualification (NVQ), in England and Wales, a work-related. competence-based qualification that shows you have the knowledge and skills to do a job effectively. NVQs represent standards that are recognised by employers throughout the UK.

non-profit sector organizations that have a main aim to provide a service rather than to make money

patisserie French pastries and cakes

plant bakery industrial bakery where large quantities of bread and cakes are produced

Scottish Vocational Qualification (SVQ), in Scotland, a work-related. competence-based qualification that shows you have the knowledge and skills to do a job effectively. SVQs represent standards that are recognised by employers throughout the UK.

silver-service waiter/waitress experienced waiter/waitress who specializes in serving food from platters directly on to the guests' plates at the table

sous chef (French for "under chef") assistant chef, the position immediately below head chef

stock taking checking the amount of supplies that the establishment has

tactful discreetly taking account of other people's feelings

technical certificate certificate earned as part of an apprenticeship through your college training. It shows that you have a broad knowledge and understanding of your area of work.

troubleshooting solving serious problems for a company or organization

turnover rate at which employees leave a workplace and are replaced by new ones

work experience placement short taster of working life within the school or college framework

Titles in the *How to get ahead in* series include:

Hardback 978 1 4062 0442 1

Hardback 978 1 4062 0443 8

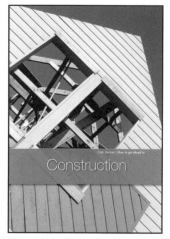

Hardback 978 1 4062 0440 7

Hardback 978 1 4062 0441 4

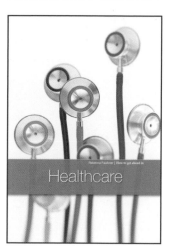

Hardback 978 1 4062 0444 5

Other titles available:

Armed and Civilian Forces	Hardback 978 1 4062 0450 6
Finance	Hardback 978 1 4062 0448 3
IT and Administration	Hardback 978 1 4062 0449 0
Leisure and Tourism	Hardback 978 1 4062 0447 6
Retail	Hardback 978 1 4062 0446 9

Find out about the other titles in this series on our website at www.raintreepublishers.co.uk